The Search and other Essays

To Victoria

The fulfillment of a dream

The Search and other Essays
Neville Goddard

CONTENTS

The Search

Once in an idle interval at sea, I meditated on "the perfect state," and wondered what I would be, were I of too pure eyes to behold iniquity, if to me all things were pure and were I without condemnation. As I became lost in this fiery brooding, I found myself lifted above the dark environment of the senses. So intense was the feeling, I felt myself a being of fire dwelling in a body of air. Voices as from a heavenly chorus, with the exaltation of those who had been conquerors in a conflict with death, were singing "He is risen He is risen," and intuitively I knew they meant me.

Then I seemed to be walking in the night. I soon came upon a scene that might have been the ancient Pool of Bethesda, for in this place lay a great multitude of impotent folk — blind, halt, withered — waiting not for the moving of the water as of tradition, but waiting for me. As I came near, without thought or effort on my part they were, one after the other, molded as by the Magician of the Beautiful. Eyes, hands, feet — all missing members— were drawn from some invisible reservoir and molded in harmony with that perfection which I felt springing within me. When all were made perfect, the chorus exulted "It is finished." Then the scene dissolved and I awoke.

I know this vision was the result of my intense meditation upon the idea of perfection, for my meditations invariably bring about union with the state contemplated. I had been so completely absorbed within the idea that for a while I had become what I contemplated, and the high purpose with which I had for that moment identified myself drew the companionship of high things and fashioned the vision in harmony with my inner nature. The ideal with which we are united works by association of ideas to awaken a thousand moods to create a drama in keeping with the central idea.

I first discovered this close relationship of moods to vision when I was aged about seven. I became aware of a mysterious life quickening within me like a stormy ocean of frightening might. I always knew when I would be united with this hidden identity, for my senses were expectant on the nights of these visitations and I knew beyond all doubt that before morning I would be alone with immensity. I so dreaded these visitations that I would lie awake until my eyes from sheer exhaustion closed. As my eyes closed in sleep, I was no longer solitary but smitten through and through with another being, and yet I knew it to be myself. It seemed older than life, yet nearer to me than my boyhood. If I tell what I discovered on these nights, I do so not to impose my ideas on others but that I may give hope to those who seek the law of life.

I discovered that my expectant mood worked as a magnet to unite me with this Greater Me, while my fears made It appear as a stormy sea. As a boy, I conceived of this mysterious self as might, and in my union with It I felt its majesty as a stormy sea which drenched me, then rolled and tossed me as a helpless wave.

As a man I conceived of It as love and myself the son of It, and in my union with It, now, what a love enfolds me! It is a mirror to all. Whatever we conceive It as being, that It is to us. I believe It to be the center through which all the threads of the universe are drawn; therefore I have altered my values and changed my ideas so that they now depend upon and are in harmony with this sole cause of all that is. It is to me that changeless reality which fashions circumstances in harmony with our concepts of ourselves.

My mystical experiences have convinced me that there is no way to bring about the outer perfection we seek other than by the transformation of ourselves. As soon as we succeed in transforming ourselves, the world will melt magically before our eyes and reshape itself in harmony with that which our transformation affirms.

Two other visions I will tell because they bear out the truth of my assertion that we, by intensity of love and hate, become what we contemplate.

Once, with closed eyes made radiant from brooding, I meditated on the eternal question, "Who Am I?" and felt myself gradually dissolve into a shoreless sea of vibrant light, imagination passing beyond all fear of death. In this state nothing existed but myself, a boundless ocean of liquid light. Never have I felt more intimate with Being. How long this experience lasted I do not know, but my return to earth was accompanied by a distinct feeling of crystallizing again into human shape.

At another time, I lay on my bed and with my eyes shut as in sleep I brooded on the mystery of Buddha. In a little while the dark caverns of my brain began to grow luminous. I seemed to be surrounded by luminous clouds which emanated from my head as fiery, pulsating rings. I saw nothing but these luminous rings for a time. Then there appeared before my eyes a rock of quartz crystal. While I gazed upon it, the crystal broke into pieces which invisible hands quickly shaped into the living Buddha. As I looked on this meditative figure, I saw that it was myself. I was the living Buddha whom I contemplated. A light like the sun glowed from this living image of myself with increasing intensity until it exploded. Then the light gradually faded and once more I was back within the blackness of my room.

Out of what sphere or treasury of design came this being mightier than human, his garments, the crystal, the light? If I saw, heard, and moved in a world of real beings when I seemed to myself to be walking in the night, when the lame, the halt, the blind were transformed in harmony with my inner nature, then I am justified in assuming that I have a more subtle body than the physical, a body that can be detached from the physical and used in other spheres; for to see, to hear, to move are functions of an organism however ethereal. If I brood over the alternative that my psychic experiences were self-begotten fantasy, no less am I moved to wonder at this mightier self who flashes on my mind a drama as real as those I experience when I am fully awake.

On these fiery meditations I have entered again and again, and I know beyond all doubt that both assumptions are true. Housed within this form of earth is a body attuned to a world of light, and I have, by intense meditation, lifted it as with a magnet through the skull of this dark house of flesh. The first time I awoke the fires within me I thought my head would explode. There was intense vibration at the base of my skull, then sudden oblivion of all. Then I found myself clothed in a garment of light and attached by a silvery elastic cord to the slumbering body on the bed. So exalted were my feelings, I felt related to the stars. In this garment I roamed spheres more familiar than earth, but found that, as on earth, conditions were molded in harmony with my nature. "Self-begotten fantasy," I hear you say. No more so than the things of earth. I am an immortal being conceiving myself as man and forming worlds in the likeness and image of my concept of self.

What we imagine, that we are. By our imagination we have created this dream of life, and by our imagination we will re-enter that eternal world of light, becoming that which we were before we imagined the world. In the divine economy nothing is lost. We cannot lose anything save by descent from the sphere where the thing has its natural life. There is no transforming power in death and, whether we are here or there, we fashion the world that surrounds us by the intensity of our imagination and feeling, and we illuminate or darken our lives by the concepts we hold of ourselves. Nothing is more important to us than our conception of ourselves, and especially is this true of our concept of the deep, hidden One within us.

Those that help or hinder us, whether they know it or not, are the servants of that law which shapes outward circumstances in harmony with our inner nature. It is our conception of ourselves which frees or constrains us, though it may use material agencies to achieve its purpose.

Because life molds the outer world to reflect the inner arrangement of our minds, there is no way of bringing about the outer perfection we seek other than by the transformation of ourselves. No help Cometh from without; the hills to which we lift our eyes are those of an inner range. It is thus to our own consciousness that we must turn as to the only reality, the only foundation on which all phenomena can be explained. We can rely absolutely on the justice of this law to give us only that which is of the nature of ourselves.

To attempt to change the world before we change our concept of ourselves is to struggle against the nature of things. There can be no outer change until there is first an inner change. As within, so without. I am not advocating philosophical indifference when I suggest that we should imagine ourselves as already that which we want to be, living in a mental atmosphere of greatness, rather than using physical means and arguments to bring about the desired change. Everything we do, unaccompanied by a change of consciousness, is but futile readjustment of surfaces. However we toil or struggle, we can receive no more than our subconscious assumptions affirm. To protest against anything which happens to us is to protest against the law of our being and our rulership over our own destiny.

The circumstances of my life are too closely related to my conception of myself not to have been launched by my own spirit from some magical storehouse of my being. If there is pain to me in these happenings, I should look within myself for the cause, for I am moved here and there and made to live in a world in harmony with my concept of myself.

Intense meditation brings about a union with the state contemplated, and during this union we see visions, have experiences, and behave in keeping with our change of consciousness. This shows us that a transformation of consciousness will result in a change of environment and behavior. However, our ordinary alterations of consciousness, as we pass from one state to another, are not transformations, because each of them is so rapidly succeeded by another in the reverse direction; but whenever one state grows so stable as to definitely expel its rivals, then that central habitual state defines the character and is a true transformation. To say that we are transformed means that ideas previously peripheral in our consciousness now take a central place and form the habitual center of our energy.

All wars prove that violent emotions are extremely potent in precipitating mental rearrangements. Every great conflict has been followed by an era of materialism and greed in which the ideals for which the conflict ostensibly was waged are submerged. This is inevitable because war evokes hate, which impels a descent in consciousness from the plane of the ideal to the level where the conflict is waged. If we would become as emotionally aroused over our ideals as we become over our dislikes, we would ascend to the plane of our ideals as easily as we now descend to the level of our hates.

Love and hate have a magical transforming power, and we grow through their exercise into the likeness of what we contemplate. By intensity of hatred we create in ourselves the character we imagine in our enemies. Qualities die for want of attention, so the unlovely states might best be rubbed out by imagining "beauty for ashes and joy for mourning" rather than by direct attacks on the state from which we would be free. "Whatsoever things are lovely and of good report, think on these things," for we become that with which we are en rapport.

There is nothing to change but our concept of self. Humanity is a single being in spite of its many forms and faces, and there is in it only such seeming separation as we find in our own being when we are dreaming. The pictures and circumstances we see in dreams are creations of our own imagination and have no existence save in ourselves. The same is true of the pictures and circumstances we see in this dream of life. They reveal our concepts of ourselves. As soon as we succeed in transforming self, our world will dissolve and reshape itself in harmony with that which our change affirms.

The universe which we study with such care is a dream, and we the dreamers of the dream, eternal dreamers dreaming non-eternal dreams. One day, like Nebuchadnezzar we shall awaken from the dream, from the nightmare in which we fought with demons, to find that we really never left our eternal home; that we were never born and have never died save in our dream.

The Seven Eyes of God

...we must go on to higher and higher levels, for that is the purpose of the teacher. I would like to look tonight into what it is to my mind, the greatest book in the world, the Bible, and show you a section with which you may not be familiar. It concerns the Seven Eyes of God, from the visions of Zechariah. He saw a stone with seven facets, and the Voice said, this is actually the seven eyes of God that reach over the entire world. For these seven eyes are really in man, for man is the earth of God. So forget this little planet and know that man is the true earth in which God is planted. These are the seven visions of God, seven increasingly clarifying visions of the Creator. The Bible names them but you must look for them.

The first appears only once in the Bible in Isaiah 14 ~ Lucifer, the morning star. And it tells how he is fallen and cut down to the ground — this shining being. All races have taught that man has fallen. It is not something that belongs to the Christian or the Jewish faiths, but all races have held this concept. So the first Eye of God is Lucifer — cut down to the ground.

The second is Molech, the strange god that demands sacrifices (Jeremiah 32). Man offers up his sons and daughters to appease this being he conceives to be God. But the Voice said, "I command them not, neither came it unto my mind, that they should do this abomination to cause Judah to sin." This Eye is in every man who thinks he has angered God and must make sacrifices to appease Him. All the wars of the world are an appeasement. The Inquisition with its tortures was an appeasement to God. The wicker baskets in which men were burned alive were an appeasement. They did it all to appease God that he might not be angry.

The third eye is Elohim, or gods, gods above and outside of man. The elements he worshipped, the stars and planets he thinks can regulate his life and influence his behavior. He turns to something outside of himself and it fails him and he cries that he is forsaken.

The fourth is Shaddai — almighty. In this eye, man seeks security and comfort. These are the governments, the mighty political machines, the rulers that man trusts, and all this fails him, too.

And then he turns to the fifth eye of Pahath, which means, "to dig a ditch or to snare animals, dig a pit." It does not mean the animals of the forest; no, it is man I bring into my little trap. Much of the world functions like that today, everywhere in every business, especially in the great advertising campaigns. These people rule like tyrants over us. Every paper, every magazine, every TV commercial has another method of trapping us into buying all these things, so many things that we never get them paid for before we have still others.

And then the sixth eye is Jehovah – Yod He Vau He – or I AM. Man finally grows out of the snaring process. He does not now have to trap anyone in the world, but only boldly assert himself. Bold inner persuasion will create the condition that I AM persuaded of. That is Jehovah, the sixth eye.

The seventh is Jesus, or "Jehovah saves," or "rescue." Where man boldly asserts himself but his heart is torn for those still asleep, and he sacrifices for the others and gives himself for the whole vast world. Not as the churches teach it, but as the mystic tells you. You will take anyone, no matter who he is or what he has done, for he is only in a state. You do not condemn anyone but you lift him out of the state, and you do it by identifying the one you would save with the idea he wants to embody, and to the degree that you are faithful to your vision of that person, he will embody his ideal and become it. That is the eye called Jesus, or the seventh eye.

There is an eighth eye, only implied in the Bible and it is veiled. On the eighth day they circumcise the child and unveil the organ of creation. There is an eye in man and Blake names it. He says, "He did not come. He hid in Albion's forest." Albion is Blake's name for universal man, male or female. This eye is hidden in "Albion's forest" – in the dark convolutions of the brain. There this eye is hiding. When you finally begin to exercise your imagination for another and actually revel in the joy of others as they become the embodiment of what they desire, and you revel in that far beyond what you would for yourself, that is the eye of Jesus. What begins to be the perfect seeing of the seventh eye of God, then something stirs, and it stirs exactly like something trying to get out of an egg. It is something trying to break through Golgotha – and Golgotha is "the skull," that is the meaning of the word. But it is held by five nails, the five senses. The five senses confine man to this world, and then he breaks loose from this skull as the seventh eye is clarified; and the eighth eye sees concrete reality for the first time in his life, and then, once seeing clearly, he never blames anyone. For with this eighth eye, he sees the perfect world. This is called circumcision or the unveiling of the perfect organ, which is man's Imagination. On the eighth day, he is circumcised. It means that the eighth eye is open. It does not open by the process of time, but only after the clarifying of the seventh eye of Jesus. Then you see that God became man, that man, awakening, may become God. God contracts Himself to this very limit of opacity, so that living in this state may be called the very grave of man, and "God enters death's door with them that enter, and lies down in the grave with them, in visions of Eternity until they awake." (Blake) And then there are these seven visions.

First — Lucifer, the fallen one.

Second — Molech, the being that demands sacrifices. They are doing that right now, only they call it Nationalism, and they offer up their sons and daughters to Molech, though the Voice said, "I do not command them to do this and cause Judah to fall into sin."

Man sickens of it and turns to the third eye or Elohim, but the stars, the planets, do not respond.

Then he turns to the fourth eye or Shaddai — Almighty, to the financial and political "gods."

And then he separates from that and digs his little pit, Pahath, and snares all the people of the world because he can outsmart them, and because of his smartness he lives very well during this little span from the cradle to the grave, and that is the fifth eye through which much of the world is seeing today.

He sickens of it, and then he finds that I AM — or Jehovah, is the only reality, or the sixth eye of God. And I build my world, as I want it and when I sicken of it, offer myself as a sacrifice for all others and give completely of myself for the good of others, and my good fortune then becomes the joy of hearing their good fortune. As it says in Job 42:5 "I heard by the hearing of my ear, but now my eye seeth Thee." Suddenly something happens within me, and the eighth eye opens and I am circumcised, in mind, not in the flesh, and as that something opens within you, you see the reason for it all, and you see that Eternity is, and you can take anyone in this world and pull him out of any state in the world. That is the eighth eye of God.

I want to share with you an experience. The true method of knowledge is through experiment. So we invite you to experiment. The true faculty of knowing is the faculty of experiencing. For, when you have had the experiences, you no longer care whether anyone else knows it or not. It does not matter. You know it, and you know that you know it. So I would like to share this with you, this experience, for when you begin to awaken, then you begin to remember. For if Christ is the center, then I can say, "Return to me the glory that was mine before the world was. I am crucified with Christ, nevertheless I live, yet not I, but Christ liveth in me, and the life I now live I live by the faith of the son of God who loved me and gave himself for me." If the center of man is Christ, and He was before the world was, then when I begin to awaken I only begin to remember. And when that happens, then the world cannot any longer teach you anything. So when man begins to awaken he does not question the things of this world; he knows they are not true. Psychologists tell us a complete understanding of a dream depends on the knowledge that you are dreaming, and then that wakes you up, for this is the only world they know. They speak of a dream state as being subjective and a deep dream state as the unconscious and doubt the worth of it all. But when you open the eighth eye you will know there are worlds within worlds and you are heirs to all of them. You can test your experiences and bring anything you want into your world and prove it.

Years ago I felt myself dreaming and I was swimming. I knew it was a dream. I looked up and saw the shore of a primitive island, not the little island where I was born, for that is well cultivated and in no way primitive, but this was primitive. I saw it was an island and I knew I was dreaming, and I saw these strange things like cement posts driven down through the water but they were in a state of decay. They could have been at one time part of a jetty. I could see this peculiar primitive beach and I prolonged the dream, for if you know you are dreaming you need not wake. Something in me began to tell me, as memory began to return, that if I would take hold of one of these pilings and not let it go, and awaken, I would awaken there. I felt it and it was solidly real, just as it would feel here, and my hand did not go through it, and I held on to it and made myself awake; and I awoke in that water on that beach and then I waded ashore. I was no more asleep in that sphere than I am here in this one.

It taught me a lesson that if I could touch anything in another world and compel myself to awaken while holding it, I would find it was real. So you do it for your world. A job you want, the home you would occupy, the marriage you want. Sit at the desk at which you would sit, live in the house you want to live in, be married to the sort of person you want to be married to, and if you hold to it in your imagination, then you will make it real in your outer world. The Ancients called this capacity the Western Gate, and tied it in with the sense of touch. If you can hang on to the thing you touch and then awaken, you will find that the thing has become real. We have it in Genesis in the story of Jacob and Esau. Isaac, the father, who was blind said, "Come close that I may touch you. Come closer." And the state symbolized by Jacob, the supplanter, was made real in place of the state that had seemed so real before, symbolized by Esau.

We are told again in Judges 17:19 how the seven locks were shaved from the head of Samson and then the Philistines came and gouged out his eyes and he was eyeless in Gaza. And they made him dance before the crowd. He asked to be taken to the temple and placed where he might touch the two middle pillars, and then he pressed and pushed and pulled down the whole thing and slew more Philistines than he had ever slain during his life. All this is symbolical of the capacity to touch. I know, for I have done it. Many a time, finding myself dreaming, I have held on to an object in the dream and found myself awakening in another world. I have also found myself in other aspects of this world. I did it in Barbados when I wished to be seen by my sister who was 2000 miles away. But whether it be in this little aspect or in another world, it does not matter, for there are infinite worlds and you are heir to all of them.

You can get all you want in this world. You can use the fifth eye or the fourth eye. All those who lead us into battle are using the second and third. Few are using the sixth and only an nth part use the seventh eye or the eye of Jesus, and not until it is used and you would rather have the good of another than your own good, and rejoice for another more than for yourself, have you really opened the seventh eye and then you are ready for the opening of the eighth eye.

The seventh eye, the eye of Jesus, has nothing to do with a man born 2000 years ago; it has everything to do with the expanding mind of man. When you exercise the seventh, then something opens. It is the eighth. But until the seventh is fully open, "he hides in the forest of Albion." He hides in the dark convolutions of the brain. It may scare you a little at first, the feeling of an electric battery moving in your head. You feel memory come back and you feel it on this side and then on that, and then you center it, and then you SEE. Something opens and you actually see a world no one else can see. The seventh eye is based purely on faith. Man does not know God will actually redeem him and he cries, "My God, why hast thou forsaken me?" And then the new world will be seen.

Man seeks security and comfort through the fourth eye. These are the dictators, the political machines, etc. They are always going to save the country, save the world, and then they are driven out — but they take a half billion dollars with them. We have seen it in this hemisphere — the very ones impoverishing the treasury that men had just called the saviors of their country.

They have not reached the sixth eye, or I AM. He who has reached that turns to no one. He knows, "I AM that I will be, I AM what I am." You can be that or anything you want. But then you go beyond it and you want nothing for yourself but only for others. Then he starts giving himself for man and then when that is completely clarified the eighth eye opens.

Look in your Bible and read the story of the unveiling of the mind of man. But it comes only after the seventh eye is exercised. So I must learn to experience feeling and touching. That is called the Western Gate, and it is closed in man, but he must learn about it, and before I close this eye he must learn much about the Western Gate, for I was told not to hold back one secret, and having had the experience of holding on to an object and awakening not on my bed at all, I must share it with you. I awake in the world where I am holding the object. I have been shut out many times from this world by holding on to an object in that world and awakening in it, and it was just as real as this, but I came back to this. I had a body here and one there. When I returned here where was that other body? Have I not many bodies, for I am scattered over all the world, and man, as he begins to awake, collects the scattered portions of himself, and then he finally finds the being that is God. You can love everyone in this world and you will find joy beyond your wildest dreams in doing good for another; when he asks of you and you, in your Imagination create, and then you have confirmation of it, and then you rejoice as God rejoices. "These things have I spoken that my joy may remain in you." For whenever anyone awakes, that is the eye of God.

So there are seven stated quite clearly and the eighth implied. I tell you that you will feel it like a chick in the egg of the skull. Christ is crucified on this cross (man) with five nails — the five senses. The same meaning is in the story of the five foolish virgins. And then he tears himself free from this cross.

Now, you catch it on the wing, but I tell you that you will discover all kinds of wonderful things in the awakening of God in man. For God became man that man may become God. So this wonderful poem that existed only for God is beginning to exist for itself. Sentients begin to appear in the poem, lifting it to higher states and we become at last creators, one of an infinite society of gods.

This eighth eye is misunderstood by the priesthoods of the world and they circumcise the child. It is the Imagination that must be unveiled, not the physical organ, and it comes only after the perfect clarity of vision through the eye of Jesus. Jesus means, "Jehovah saves." Not one is lost. He has fallen into a state, but you, through the eye of Jesus, save him. You ask him, "What do you want?" and see that condition real for him, and then seeing it embody itself, you rejoice that one has been lifted out of the mire. You do it over and over, and then your head becomes alive and you feel electric currents through it, and yet you will know what you should do, just as a chick knows what to do. It pecks its way out. And then the place where the skull grew together after birth becomes awake again, and you see another world, and you see the world was perfectly made and every state is perfect, and then you will know that you are awake to play beautifully on this eternal world, to bring out these beautiful combinations made by your Father.

If tonight's talk seems different from what you expected, then nothing is more practical than the sixth eye. You can make your world what you want it to be by the sixth eye; in fact the fifth has done it. You can snare all kinds of people in your little traps. Read the morning papers. Every ad is to snare us into emptying our pockets, and they will be thrilled that they can do it. Every year we find new traps to get what we have. We have new forms of credit. No one dies leaving anything behind any more. The whole vast thing is a trap. It has become the way of life, the fifth eye.

But then come the sixth and the seventh and then the eighth; and when the eighth opens you forgive everyone in the world, no matter what he has done. You, as man, have gone through every eye. You have worshipped Elohim and sacrificed to Molech.

But when the eighth opens, you will know that nothing displeases your Father but unbelief. Sin does not displease him. The priesthoods of the world tell you sin displeases him, but only disbelief displeases him, for they that come to him must believe in him. Anything you can believe is an image of truth. Could you believe that someone in dire need is now well taken care of? Then he can become as you see him. But sin does not displease your Father. It means, "to miss the mark," and He comes to the world to show everyone how not to miss the mark. If I do miss the mark, He makes a greater effort to show me how not to miss marks.

Hebrews 11 — "Those who come to Him must believe that He is, and that He is the rewarder of them that seek..." So seek Him first and then all these things will be added.

So there are these eight eyes in man. The eighth hides in the forest of Albion, or the dark convolutions of the brain. Breathing won't bring it out, or diets, or Yoga exercises will not do it. He will come out only when, as you look through the seventh eye, which is the vision of Jesus, you see only the good of another and glory in that beyond what is only for yourself. Then you will begin to see through the eighth eye of God.

Use the seventh eye consciously and take every person regardless of color, race or creed and ask of him only, "What do you want?" For in Him there is neither Greek nor Jew, nor bond nor free. So you take everyone, for he has only fallen into a state and you single out that individual's request and persuade yourself that he is now the embodiment of the ideal that he wants to embody and to the degree that you use the seventh eye will the eighth come out of the "forest of Albion." The opening of the eighth eye is actually the second coming of Jesus. For when the seventh becomes perfectly clear, then the eighth will open, as if it were released from the tomb, and then you see as God.

One cannot be born a Christian. If you are not using the seventh eye, you are not a Christian. If you are the Pope, you are using the fourth eye and all the priesthoods of the world use the fourth eye. So-called almighty powers all use the fourth eye. But you must use the eye of Jesus. Jesus is the eye of God that sacrifices itself for the whole vast world. He gives himself for every being in the world, seeing for them their ideal, their perfect state.

Now let us go into the silence.

Awakened Imagination

As you have heard, this morning's subject is "Awakened Imagination." It is my theme for the entire series of nineteen lectures. Everything is geared towards the awakening of the imagination. I doubt if there is any subject on which clear thinking is more rare than the imagination. The word itself is made to serve all kinds of ideas. many of them directly opposed to one another. But here this morning I hope to convince you that this is the redeeming power in man. This is the power spoken of in the Bible as the Second Man. "the Lord from Heaven." This is the same power personified for us as a man called Christ Jesus.

In the ancient text it was called Jacob, and there are numberless names in the Bible all leading up and culminating in the grand flower called Christ Jesus.

It may startle you to identify the central figure of the Gospels as human imagination, but I am quite sure before the series is over, you will be convinced that this what the ancients intended that we should know, but man has misread the Gospels as history and biography and cosmology, and so completely has gone asleep as to the power within himself.

Now this morning I have brought you the means by which this mighty power in us may be awakened. I call it the art of revision. I take my day and I review it in my mind's eye. I start with the first incident in the morning. I go through the day; when I come to any scene in my unfolding day that displeased me, or if it didn't displease me if it was not as perfect as I thought it could have been, I stop right there and I revise it. I re-write it, and after I have re-written it so that it conforms to the ideal I wished I had experienced, then I experience that in my imagination as though I had experienced it in the flesh. I do it over and over until it takes on the tone of reality, and experience convinces me that that moment that I have revised and relived will not recede into my past. It will advance into my future to confront me as I have revised it. If I do not revise it, these moments, because they never recede and they always advance, will advance to confront me perpetuating that strange, unlovely incident. But if I refuse to allow the sun to descend upon my wrath, so that at the end of a day I never accept as final the facts of the day, no matter how factual they are, I never accept them, and revising it I repeal the day and bring about corresponding changes in my outer world.

Now, not only will this art of revision accomplish my every objective, but as I begin to revise the day it fulfills its great purpose and its great purpose is to awaken in me the being that men call Christ Jesus, that I call my wonderful human imagination, and when it awakens it is the eye of God and it turns

inward into the world of thought and there I see that what formerly I believed
to exist on the outside really exists within myself. No matter what it is, I then
discover that the whole of Creation is rooted in me and ends in me as I am
rooted in and end in God. And from that moment on I find my real purpose
in life and my real purpose is simply to do the will of Him that sent me, and the
will of Him that sent me is this —that of all that he has given me I shall lose
nothing but raise it up again.

And what did he give me? He gave me every experience in my life. He gave me
you. Every man, woman and child that I meet is a gift to me from my Father,
but they fell in me because of my attitude towards society, because of my attitude
towards myself. When I begin to awaken and the eye opens and I see the whole
is myself made visible, I then must fulfill my real purpose, which is the will of
Him that sent me, and the Will is to raise up those that I allowed in my
ignorance when I slept to descend within me. Then starts the real art of revision;
to be the man, regardless of your impressions of that man, regardless of the facts
of the case that are all staring you in the face, it is your duty when you become
awakened to lift him up within yourself and you will discover that he was never
the cause of your displeasure. When you look at him and you are displeased,
look within and you will find the source of the displeasure. It did not originate
there.

Now let me give you a case history to illustrate this point. I know a few of you
were at the banquet and maybe a few of you heard me last Thursday on T. V.
but I doubt in this audience of say twenty-three or twenty-four hundred of us,
that more than say a hundred and fifty heard it, and even if you heard it you can
hear it time and time again for it is this, that if you hear it will cause you to act
upon it because as I told you, and I think I did last Sunday, but if I didn't let me
tell you now; if you attended the entire nineteen and you became saturated with
all that I have to tell you, so that you had all the knowledge you think it takes
to achieve your objectives, and you did not apply what you received, it would
avail you nothing; but a little knowledge which you carry out in action, you will
find to be far more profitable than much knowledge which you neglect to carry
out in action. So by repeating this case history this morning, though say a
hundred or two hundred of you have heard it, it will help you to remember you
must do something about it.

This past May in New York City, there sat a lady who had been coming for
years and I made a simple observation that people must become doers of the
word and not mere hearers only. For if a man only hears it and never applies
what he hears he will never really prove or disprove what he has heard; and then
I told the story of a lady who had only heard me three or four times and how

she transformed the life of another, and this lady hearing what one who came only three times and this miracle took place in her life, she went home determined that she would really apply what she had heard over the years, and this is what she did.

Two years before, after a violent quarrel, she was ordered out of her son's home by her daughter-in-law. Her son said "Mother, you need no proof from me that I love you: it's obvious: I think I have proven that every day of my life, but if that is Mary's decision, and I regret it, it must be my decision, for I love Mary and we live in the same house and it is our house: it is our little family, and I am sorry she feels this way about it, but you know these little things that culminate in an explosion as took place today. If that is her decision, it is mine." That was two years ago. She went home and she realized that night after night for over two years she had allowed the sun to descend upon her wrath. She thought of this wonderful family that she loved and felt herself ostracized from it, expelled from the home of her son. She did nothing about revising it and yet I had been talking revision to my New York audience for the past year.

This is what she did now. She knew the morning's mail brought nothing. This was a Wednesday night. There had been no correspondence in two years. She had sent her grandson at least a dozen gifts in the two years. Not one was ever acknowledged. She knew they had been received for she had insured many of them; so she sat down that night and mentally wrote herself two letters—one from her daughter-in-law, expressing a great kindness for her, saying that she had been missed in the home and asking her when she was coming to see them; then she wrote one from her grandson in which he said "Grandmother, I love you." Then came a little expression of thanks for the last birthday present, which was in April, and then came a feeling of sadness rather because he hadn't seen her and begging her to come and see him soon.

These two short notes she memorized and then, as she was about to sleep, she took her imaginary hands and held these letters and she read them mentally to herself until they woke in her the feeling of joy because she had heard from her family; that she was wanted once more. She read these letters over and over feeling the joy that was hers because she had received them and fell asleep in her project. For seven nights this lady read these two letters. On the morning of the eighth day she received the letter: on the inside there were two letters—one from her grandson and one from her daughter-in-law. These letters were identical with the letters she had mentally written to herself seven days before. Where was the estrangement? Where was the conflict? Where was the source of the displeasure that was like a running sore over two years? When man's eye is opened he realizes all that he beholds, though it appears without, it is within—within one's own imagination, of which this world of mortality is but a shadow.

She gave me permission to tell that story. When I told it, and we came to the period of questions and answers, there was a strange reaction from that crowd. They wondered what joy life would hold for any of us if we had to write our own letters; if we had to do everything to ourselves that seemingly is done in joy; that seemingly is spontaneous coming from another; but I don't want to write myself a love letter from my wife, or my sweetheart or my friend. I want that one to feel this way towards me and to express it unknown to me that I may receive a surprise in life.

Well, I am not denying that sleeping man firmly believes that is the way things happen. When a man awakes he realizes that everything he encounters is apart of himself, and what he does not now comprehend, he knows, because the eye is opened, that it is related by affinity to some as yet unrealized force in his own being; that he wrote it but he has forgotten it, that he slapped himself in the face but he has forgotten it; that within himself he started the entire unfolding drama, and he looks out upon a world, and it seems strange to him, because most of us in our sleep are totally unaware of what we are doing from within ourselves.

What that lady did, every man and woman in this audience today can do. It will not take you years to prove it; what I tell you now may startle you; it may seem to be bordering on insanity for the insane believe in the reality of subjective states and the sane man only believes in what the senses will allow, what they will dictate, and I'm going to tell you when you begin to awake, you assert the supremacy of imagination and you put all things in subjection to it. You never again bow before the dictates of facts and accept life on the basis of the world without. To you Truth is not confined by facts but by the intensity of your imagination. So here we find the embodiment of Truth, which I say is human imagination, standing in the world drama before the embodiment of reason personified as Pontius Pilate. And he is given the authority to question truth and they ask him, "What is the truth?" and Truth remains silent. He refuses to justify any action of his; he refuses to justify anything that was done to him, for he knows no man cometh unto me save I call him: no man takes away my life, I lay it down myself.

You didn't choose me, I have chosen you. For here is Truth seeing nothing hereafter in pure objectivity, but seeing everything subjectively related to himself and he the source of all the actions that take place within his world; so Truth remains absolutely silent and says nothing when reason questions him concerning the true definition of Truth. Because when the eye opens it knows that what is an idea to sleeping man is a fact to the awakened imagination, an objective fact, not an idea. I entertain the idea of a friend and I make some wonderful concept of him in my mind's eye and when I sleep it seems to be a wish, it seems to be the longing of my heart, but purely subjective, just an idea. And the eye within me opens, and he stands before me embodying the quality that I desired in my sleep to see him express. So what is an idea to sleeping man, the unawakened imagination, is an objective reality to awakened imagination.

Now, this exercise calls for, I would say, the active, voluntary use of imagination as against the passive, involuntary acceptance of appearances. We never accept as true and as final anything unless it conforms to the ideal we desire to embody within our world, and we do exactly what the grandmother did. But now we start it and we do it daily. You may get your results tomorrow; it may come the day after; it may come in a week, but I assure you they will come.

You do not need some strange laboratory, like our scientists, to prove or disprove this theory. Here in 1905 a young man startled the scientific world with his equation that no one could even test. It is said not six men lived who could understand his equation. It was 14 years later before Lord Rutherford could devise the means to test that equation and he found that it was true, not 100%, because he did not have the means at his hand to really give it a complete test. It was another 14 years before further tests could be made. And you know the results of that equation that Einstein gave us in 1905. For today man, not knowing the power of his own imagination, stands startled at the results of that unlocking of energy. But he was the man who said, and I put it in the first page of my new book—"Imagination is more important than knowledge"

That was Albert Einstein. Imagination is more important than knowledge. For if man accepts as final the facts that evidence bears witness to, he will never exercise this God-given means of redemption, which is his imagination. Now I'm going to ask you to test this: you will not take the three weeks that I am here to prove it or disprove it, but the knowledge of it cannot prove itself, only the application of that knowledge can prove it or disprove it. I know from experience you cannot disprove it. Take an objective, take a job, take some conversation with your boss, take an increase in salary. You say well, the job doesn't allow it, or maybe the Union will not allow it. I don't care what doesn't allow it.

Yesterday morning's mail brought me one, where, in San Francisco, this captain, a pilot, and he writes me that I saw him backstage after one of my meetings, and there he said, "But Neville, you are up against a stone wall. I am a trained pilot; I have gone all over the world, all over the seven seas; I'm a good pilot and I love the sea, not a thing in this world I want to do but go to sea; yet they restrict me to certain waters because of seniority. No matter what argument I give them the Union is adamant and they have closed the book on my request." I said, "I don't care what they have done, you are transferring the power that rightfully belongs to God, which is your own imagination, to the shadow you cast upon the screen of space.

"So here, we are in this room; need it remain a room? Can't you use your imagination to call this a bridge. This is now a bridge and I am a guest on the bridge of your ship, and you are not in waters restricted by the Union; you are in waters that you desire to sail your ship. Now close your eyes and feel the rhythm of the ocean and feel with me and commune with me and tell me of your joy in first proving this principle. and secondly in being at sea where you want to be. He is now in Vancouver on a ship bringing a load of lumber down to Panama. He has a complete list that will take him through the year what this man has to do. He is going into waters legitimately that the Union said he could not go. This doesn't dispense with unions, but it does not put anyone in our place — no one, kings, queens, presidents, generals, we take no one and enthrone him and put him beyond the power that rightfully belongs to God. So I will not violate the law but things will open that I will never devise.

I will sit in the silence and within myself I will revise the picture. I will hear the very man who told me "No, and that's final" and hear him tell me yes, and a door opens. I don't have to go and pull strings or pull any wires whatsoever. I call upon this wonderful power within myself, which man has forgotten completely because he personified it and called it another man, even though it is a glorious picture of a man but that is not the man: the real man is not in some other world. When religion speaks, if it's a real religion, it speaks not of another world; it speaks of another man that is latent but unborn in every man that has attunement with another world of meaning, so that man sat and he tuned in with another world of meaning and brought into being a power that he allowed to go to sleep because he read the laws of man too well. He accepted as final the dictate of facts for they read him the by-laws, they read him the laws of the Union. And here today he is flying the ocean as he wants to do it. The grandmother is no longer locked out from the home she loved, but she is in communion, but she was locked out by herself for two years. And he was locked out by himself for well over 18 months, and burning up day after day allowing the sun to descend upon his wrath when he had the power within himself and the key to unlock every door in the world.

I say to each and everyone of you I wouldn't take from you your outer comfort, your religion, for all these things are like toys for sleeping man, but I come to awaken within you that which when it awakes it sees an entirely different world. It sees a world that no man when he sleeps could ever see, and then he starts to raise within himself every being that God gave him; and may I tell you God gave you everyman that walks the face of the earth. He also gave it for this purpose that nothing is to be discarded. Everyone in the world must be redeemed and your individual life is the process by which this redemption is brought to pass.

So we don't discard because the thing is unpleasant, we revise it; revising it we repeal it, and as we repeal it it projects itself on the screen of space bearing witness to the power within us, which is our wonderful human imagination. And I say human advisedly—some would have me say the word divine. The very word itself means nothing to man. He has pushed it off from himself completely and divorced himself from the thing that he now bows before and calls by other names. I say human imagination. As Blake said "Rivers, mountains, cities, villages all are human." When the eye opens you see them in your own bosom, in your own wonderful bosom they all exist, they are rooted there. Don't let them fall and remain fallen; lift them up for the will of my Father is this, that of all that he has given me I should lose nothing but raise it up again, and I raise it up every time I revise my concept of another and make him conform to the ideal image I myself would like to express in this world. When I do unto him what I would love the world to do unto me, and see in me I am lifting him up.

And may I tell you what happens to that man when he does it? First of all, he is already turned around within himself. He no longer sees the world in pure objectivity, but the whole world subjectively related to himself, and hang it upon himself. As he lifts it up do you know he blooms within himself. When this eye of mine was first opened I beheld man as the prophet saw him. I saw him as a tree walking: some were only like little antlers of a stag, others were majestic in their foliage, and all that were really awake were in full bloom. These are the trees in the garden of God. As told us in the old ancient way of revision in the 61st chapter of the Book of Isaiah—"Go and give beauty for ashes, go and give joy for mourning, give the spirit of praise for the spirit of heaviness, that they may become trees of righteousness, plantings to the glory of God."

That is what everyman must do, that's revision. I see ash when the business is gone; you can't redeem it, you can't lift it up, conditions are bad and the thing has turned to ash. Put beauty in its place; see customers, healthy customers, healthy in finances, healthy in the attitude towards you, healthy in every sense of the word. See them loving to shop with you if you are a shopkeeper; if you are a factory worker, don't see anything laying you off, lift it up, put beauty in the place of ash, for that would be ash if you were laid off with a family to feed. If someone is mourning, put joy in the place of mourning; if someone is heavy of spirit, put the spirit of praise in place of the spirit of heaviness, and as you do this and revise the day you turn around, and turning around you turn up, and all the energies that went down when you were sound asleep and really blind now turn up and you become a tree of righteousness, a planting to the glory of God. For I have seen them walking this wonderful earth, which is really the Garden; we have shut ourselves out by our concept of self and we have turned down.

As told us in the Book of Daniel, we were once this glorious tree and it was felled to the very base, and what formerly sheltered the nations and fed the nations and comforted the bird and gave some comfort to the animals from the sun of the day, of the heat of the day; and suddenly some voice said from within, "Let it lie, let it remain as it is, but do not disturb the roots; I will water it with the dew of heaven and as I water it with the dew of heaven it will once more grow again, but this time it will consciously grow, it will know what it really is and who it is. In its past it was majestic but it had no conscious knowledge of its majesty, and I felled it — that was the descent of man. And now, he will once more spring from within himself and he will be a tree walking, a glorious, wonderful tree.

Now to those who are sound asleep this may seem to you too startling: this may be just as startling as Einstein's equation was; that was startling too. But I tell you I've seen it and I see it— men are destined to be trees in the garden of God. They are planted on earth for a purpose and they don't always remain men, they are transformed as they turn in and turn up. This is the true meaning of the transfiguration. There is a complete metamorphosis taking place like the grub into the butterfly. You don't remain what you appear to be when man is asleep, and there is no more glorious picture in the world than to see this living animated human being, for every branch within him is represented by an extension of himself called another, and when he lifts the other up that branch not only comes into leafage but it blossoms and the living human blossoms that blossom upon the tree of man who awakens.

So that's my message for you this year; I'll give it to you to stir into being that which sleeps in you, for the son of God sleeps in man and the only purpose of being is to awaken him. So it is not to awaken this, nice as it appears to be, but this man of sense—is only a casing: it is called the first man, but the first shall be last and the last shall be first. So that which comes into being second, like Jacob coming second from his mother's womb, he takes precedence over his brother Esau who came first. Esau was the one like this, he was made of skin and hair, and Jacob was made a smooth skinned lad, but that one that comes second suddenly becomes the lord of all the nations and that one sleeps in everyman born of woman, and it is the duty of a teacher or a true religion to awaken that man, not to talk of another world, not to make promises to be fulfilled beyond the grave, but to tell him as he awakens now he is in heaven and the kingdom is come now, this day, on earth. For as he awakens he revises his day and he repeals his day and projects a more beautiful picture onto the screen of space.

You Can Forgive Sin

"You Can Forgive Sin." That, to most people, will be blasphemy as you will hear later on, quoting from scripture. It is so common among all of us to ascribe our ills and troubles to outward things - like the present conditions of the world, to our environment, or simply to things. And these things may be things that are absent from our world, or things we have in our world, but still things, while all along the real cause of our ills is sin. So we are told he was called Jesus because he came to save men from their sins; his only concern was the saving of men from sin.

Now what is sin? Sin means "missing the mark," missing the road, "missing the goal" in life. If you haven't a mark you can't sin. If you have a goal in this world and do not realize it and miss it, then you have sinned. So his purpose is to show man how not to sin in this world. No condemnation. Tell me you sin - tell me your goal, and I will tell you God's word. That is what he said. He has come only to show man how not to miss his objective in this world.

Now we turn to Mark 2:3 - or the same thing with a different twist in Matthew 9:2. It is the story of the paralytic. We are told he was preaching the word, that is, the story of salvation, and they brought in a paralytic carried by four men; and seeing their faith, he said to the paralytic: "My son, your sins are forgiven." (2:5) And scribes sitting around thought in their heart, "Why does this man speak thus? It is blasphemy! Who can forgive sins but God alone?" And discerning in their hearts what they contemplated, he said, "Why do you question thus in your hearts? Which is easier, to say to the paralytic, 'Your sins are forgiven,' or to say 'Rise, take up your pallet and walk?'" So he said to him, "Take up your bed and walk and go home" and he rose and went on his way. Then we are told," . . . they were all amazed and glorified God . . ." who had given such authority to men, for it was a man who did it. We are that man. It is to us that this authority to forgive sin has been given. And the world thought they were simply the exclusive power of some being outside ofman. Read it inMark 2 and Matthew 9.

Now what is this ability to forgive sin? We know that "sin" means missing the mark. The one that forgave it called himself, "The Truth." He said: "I amthe Truth. If you know my word and abide in my word, then you will know the Truth and the Truth will set you free." (John 8:31, 32) For the whole story begins he was teaching the truth - the word. Now, he calls himself "the truth." If I said to you tonight, what would you like to be in this world? And you name it - I would like to be_____ (no matter what it is) and I turned to you and said:

You are that, you are it; right now you are it — you would say: I am it? I can't believe it! Then you are denying the truth. He said: "I amthe Truth" - I AM everything in this world; everything man can ever imagine, I AM. So, you imagine what you would like to be. If you cannot remain faithful and loyal to that vision of yourself, then you are sinning. Not to sin is to have a goal. What would it be like? If I remain faithful to that vision as though it were true, no power in this world could stop me from realizing it - but no power. I could realize it. How? Don't ask me. But if it took the entire world of three billion to play parts to aid me in the fulfillment of my vision, they would play it without knowing they had played it. It would make no difference if they knew or did not know. They would have to contribute to the fulfillment of my vision, if I remain loyal to that vision.

So, what would it be like if I were the man I would like to be? If I said to you tonight: is there a man in this room who is rich? And no one said, I am rich - that is not your goal, and if it is, you are missing the mark. If there is a man in this room - general man - who is known, who is contributing to the world's good, and no one replies, I am he, then either it is not your goal — or if it is your goal, you are missing it. So the name is "I AM he," as told in John 8:24: "I told you that you would die in your sins, for you will die in your sins unless you believe that I am he." This is not a man talking to me. This is taking place in the depths of the soul of man. If you don't believe now that I AM the one that I would be, then you are missing your goal and you are sinning. So it does not come from without; it is not caused by anything on the outside at all. My health problems are not caused by conditions and by environment, or anything else; it is caused only by sin - and sin is missing the mark. There is only one being - one person in the world - who can hit that mark, and it is God. God forgives sin, as told us in Isaiah: "I am the Lord, I am thy Savior, and there is no other savior." "I, I am the Lord, and besides me there is no savior. No one has formed before me or no one will be formed after me. I am the Savior." (Isaiah 43:3; 43:11)

You will be saved from what you are. There is only one being in the world that can save you, and that Being is "I AM." So, you save yourself. What would it be like were it true - if I were now the man or woman I would like to be? Assume it and dare to believe it and walk as though it were true, and no power in this world can stop it - but no power! There is no one greater than God. Say, "I am" - that is God. You stand in the presence of a being and because he has a little tag - or because he is the Premier of a certain country, or Queen, or President of a certain land, you think he is greater than you are? You are missing the mark. You can't stand in the presence of anyone who is greater than you, if you know who you are. You are not going to lord it over them, knowing, but no one will be smaller, either – all are God. Then you are told to go and tell them. (Ezekiel 3:18, 33:8) – "go and tell them. If you do not tell them, and they sin and you do not tell them they will die in their sin, but their blood will be upon your head. If you tell them and they do not repent, they will die in their sin, but the blood will not be upon your head. So tell them." So Jesus is made to confess that he told them, that the blood might not be upon his head.

I Acts 20:26, 27 Paul makes the confession:" . . . for I did not shrink from declaring to you the whole counsel of God. Therefore I testify to you this day that I am innocent of the blood of all of you, for I did not shrink from declaring to you the whole counsel of God." He told them that, that he may not carry that secret to the grave and not share it with the world. So I have told the mall, that this is a principle that cannot fail.

Now let us come back to the paralytic. You came here tonight on your own steam, as it were. If I tell you we are the paralytic of scripture, you will be surprised. They were brought into the place by four men. Do you know who the four men are? The ancients always called us by the four senses – the four rivers that ran out of Eden. They did not speak of five, they spoke always of four. They joined taste and touch together because they depended upon contact. To taste something or touch something, it must be contacted. But they separated sight, sound, and scent. These three were separate in the great symbolism of scripture. But taste and touch were joined. They called them the four senses, and we came here tonight borne by these four men. I know my bank balance, and in two weeks Uncle Sam wants part of what I earned. I do not even know Uncle Sam. They tell me he exists somewhere, but I do not know where; so I am supposed to pay on the 15th of next month "x" number of dollars. Regardless of how I live, I must save something to pay him. It is the land of Caesar, I am fully aware of that. I can see my bank balance. I know what it is in my world. I can take my senses and bring it to play on what is taking place.

I was brought here tonight on the shoulders of these men. He tells me: your sins are forgiven, and, walk. How can I do it, knowing what I must pay on the 15th, knowing what I must do between now and the 15th? How will I do it? Your sins are forgiven, but who can forgive but God? Only God can forgive, and God is I AM. All right, I will now see the world as I would see it were it now May 1st and all things behind me, completely paid, paid in full.

Suppose I was unemployed. I was brought here tonight on the backs of these men. I know I have rent to pay and food to buy – all of these things – and he tells me my sins were forgiven, to rise and take up my bed and walk! How? I was brought in here on the backs of four men and called upon to rise – ignore these four and walk on my own steam now. Don't walk based on what the four allow me to see, to hear, and smell, and to be. Walk out of here unaided by these four. Walk on my own. How? I ignore the evidence of the senses. They brought me in here. I completely ignore what they tell me I really have in this world, and I see what I would like to see and assume things are what I would like them to be, and influence every being in the world to play their part to fulfill what I am assuming that I am in this world. I came in a paralytic, and walk out on my own steam. That is the story.

Every being in the world is called upon to rise and walk out, for he forgives your sin. He comes into the world only to free man of sin, no matter what you have ever done in this world. Don't look back on things as they are; look on things as they ought to be, the man or woman you would like to be, and assume that you are and see that only. And then you will know what it is to forgive sin. Who forgives? God forgives. He forgave you. I assumed. Who assumed? I assumed, that is - God. "I AM" is His name. I AM assuming I AM the man I would like to be. That is God. I begin to name it and walk in that state, and that is God. There is nothing but God. Forget what you have done. or what you are seemingly doing, and dream of the man or woman you would like to be and dare to assume you are it.

Now we are told by the great Blake: "The spirit of Jesus is continual forgiveness of sin" - forgiveness of sin every moment of time. Tonight when we go into the silence we can sit here for a minute and forgive each other. Suppose I could hear everyone here rise and tell the most fantastic story in the world about themselves or a friend, or a relative - or someone. Suppose I, really wanting it to be told from this platform, sit in the silence and listen to that and that only - the most fantastic story in the world that you could tell me individually. If I walk out of here tonight convinced that I heard it and remain loyal to what I have imagined I heard, I must hear it - no power can stop it, if I remain loyal. If anyone says it has not worked, I am not asking any questions, but as far as I am concerned, it has worked. I am sure when I know the vision I am holding for you "has its own appointed hour, it will ripen and it will flower. If it seems long in coming, wait. It is sure, it will not be late." If I actually assume things are as I would like them to be of every being here, and I remain loyal, I either know the story is true or it is false. I know it is true. It can't fail. There is no power in the world to make it fail.

Another word for sin in the Bible is "trespass." In our wonderful Lord's Prayer, "Forgive us our trespasses as we forgive those who trespass against us." It is a minor infraction of this principle. "Trespassing" means an individual lapse, a temporary relapse. You and I begin to discuss a personality. What amI doing? He is only in a state. So, I must think he is unemployed when you and I get into the discussion. I discuss a man who is unemployed and we see him as unemployed and begin to say: Well, conditions are bad, or maybe he was not good enough for the job, and you and I are discussing a man that is unemployed and we see only the state. I am trespassing. He is in the state. But I may fall into this little trap. We all do it, every day, all day long.

We read the paper, and a man is called a great man because he happens to be President, or maybe some other person in this world. We read some columnist about him and you are carried away with what the columnist tells us, and suddenly we begin to think as he would have you think, and you are trespassing. "Lord, forgive us our trespasses as we forgive those who trespass against us." It is a slight departure from our goal. We are moved aside by what we read, or heard, or saw in this world. So, that is trespassing. So, I discuss someone who cannot find the job - well, will he qualify? I am asking all these things, and they are irrelevant to this principle. Not with this principle do they have any value whatsoever. What does he want? He wants a job. And how much does he want? He names a figure. Suppose that he had what he wanted - then let me assume it is true and I begin to see the world as I would see it for him were it true and feel the joy that would be mine were he now gainfully employed, earning that sort of money. This is either true, or it is false. I tell you: it is true.

If today you and I can say The Lord's Prayer - but really say it - and ask forgiveness for our trespasses and let him show mercy for having gotten off the mark as it were. Read the story. He is brought in on the backs of four men. He himself had no faith. But in spite of what they knew, there was still a certain faith, and they brought him into the presence of God, knowing God could forgive sin. And he said: "Because of your faith" - he speaks now to those who brought him; he did not speak to the man at first, then he addresses the paralytic: "My son, your sins are forgiven you." Here, a vicarious faith. So, I can have the faith for you if you do not have it for yourself. You can have it for me if I don't have it for myself. Quite often vicarious faith is easier than the direct faith. If I can turn to you, if you really believe an imaginal act is a fact, and you could actually believe I am now what I would like to be, and although at the moment I doubt and am not faithful, you can say — in spite of myself you can pull me out — for a minute I would know faith. Those who brought him on their backs showed faith in bringing him into the presence of God. God commended them for their faith. And he turned to the paralytic and said: "My son, your sins are forgiven." Those who heard thought it blasphemy. Who could forgive sin but God alone?

He did forgive sin, for he was the "I AM." "Unless you believe I AM he, you die in your sins." So, I ask you tonight, turn to your neighbor, and maybe you can hear what the other wants and rejoice in their good fortune, and they can rejoice in your good fortune Actually feel it is true, and see the world as it would be were they what they wanted to be - and they will become it.

So, this is the story of our ability to forgive sin. They were afraid when they saw what happened and then they crucified God because he had given such authority to men. We are told: "If you retain it, it is retained. If you release it, it is released." I see a man and judge him by my senses. I retain it. But I could release him by seeing him standing on his own feet and moving in this world in a glorious manner. So the material I formerly would discard as no good, I don't discard anymore. I take it and use it. I take the same man that formerly I would discard and see him as gainfully employed, loved, and loving, and believe that the thing I am seeing for him is true; and to the degree I am faithful to the concept for him, it becomes true in this world.

That is our power. We have power to forgive sin. If you don't have a mark in this world, you can't sin. If hasn't a thing to do with moral issues. No. Do you have a goal? Do you have some objective in this world? Then this is how you realize it. Suppose it were true. In Romans 8:4:". . .walk not according to the flesh but according to the Spirit." Flesh would be my senses. My senses deny that I am what I would like to be. Let us not walk by flesh — let us walk by the Spirit. Spirit is to see it in my imagination as though it were true. Tonight I may go home to find an empty cupboard or a notice at my door: "Tomorrow, or else." It is all right. If I believe what I am imagining, it would make no difference what threat was given me - if I really believed. "Now believe it," we are told. If you believe it, it will crystallize into fact. It does not really matter what threat at the moment my senses tell me —I have to ignore it. I have to ignore the four who brought me in this place. I will not now be borne anymore by these four. I will simply walk by spirit and not by flesh.

So, I ask you to try it. If you try it you can't fail and — realizing your objective, may I also ask you to share it with me so that I may tell it to you.

About three months ago a man sat in this audience, and he wrote me a sweet, wonderful letter which I received this morning. He expected a big bonus. He had worked hard with all the promise, and one who was never on the job, but by his estimate "one of the girl friends of the boss" — she got the big bonus. He, who had done all the work, got practically nothing. So, he and I agreed mentally that he would have the most wonderful job, with more money and everything. This is now going on April. It seemed a long while, but today he is on the job, with more money than he had - more than he expected - more responsibility and opportunity, and everything. I remained faithful to that letter I knew would come when he would write it. And all I did, I heard him tell me (mentally) what he would tell me were it true, and I never wavered.

So, I only ask you to be as faithful to any imaginal state in this world, no matter what it is. In everyone God resides. Everyone has to say, "I am." That is God. I am Einstein, I am Neville. I AM is God. Neville is a tiny thing resting on the foundation that is God. I am rich - that is a tiny thing on the foundation of God, and God is Infinity, God is Everything. Therefore, whatever you say, before you say it, you say, "I am" - and you listen and you notice the four men who brought him in, brought him in paralyzed. He isn't that at all. But they deny it - the four senses are bringing him in and the four senses deny it, the four senses ignore it.

When you call on the name of God, you don't say in the name of God, so-and-so; you ask with the name of God, and to ask with the name of God you say: "I AM wealthy, healthy, secure" — then you believe it. If you ask with the name of God and believe it mentally, you will see the world as you have never seen it before you made the claim, and remain faithful to that claim and it must crystallize in your world.

This is this principle and it goes with every being in the world, regardless of nationality or pigment of skin. It is allGod. Everyone has to say, "I am" before he says, "I am- this . . ." "I am a man" — you say, "I am" before you said, "man." "I am American," "I am Indian," "I am Japanese," "I am Chinese." What kind of a being would you like to be? You name it. "I AM" is doing it. Take this fabulous world of ours and take all your dreams and put the mon the only foundation - no other foundation than God - and God is I AM.

So, the paralytic came here tonight in all of us, and we were borne on the backs of four men, and the four are our four senses: sight, scent, [sound], taste, and touch. Taste and touch are joined into one because they depend on contact. These are the four streams - the four rivers of life that come from the Garden of Eden. Any moment of time we are in the presence of I AM! Let him forgive me my sin. I forgive myself by daring to assume I am what I would like to be and assuming that I walk in that assumption and it crystallizes into fact. No power in the world can stop it - but none!

When we speak of sin, don't let anyone scare you about sin. He comes to forgive the sinner. His only interest is in the sinner. The so-called moral violations - forget it! I do not ask you to violate them, but forget them. Everything will be ironed out. It is my duty. Through the consciousness of Paul, Ezekiel, Jesus - "If I don't tell you what I know of God's law, then your sin is upon my head; but if I tell you and you still will not believe me, you will die in your sin, but your blood will not be upon my head." So Paul said: "I will tell them. I have declared the entire counsel of God to them, so I am innocent of their blood." Infinite states. A man falls into a state and so he is in the state, but he is not the state. Take him out of the state by saying while he is in the state: "What would you like?" and he names the state that he would like to enter. And you put him into that state by asking what it would be like if he were now the thing he would like to be; and you remain faithful – leaving him where he is – but you remain faithful to this concept and he comes out of it. On reflection, he might say: "It would have happened anyway." It is all right – you know. Tell everyone the story, and tell them it is entirely up to them. If they believe it – as we are told: "If you do not believe I AM He you die in your sins." (John 8)When you read it, you might think a man is telling you: I am God, and you are not. The whole story is taking place in the soul of man. That is the story.

Now he tells us the truth: "You shall know the Truth and the Truth will set you free." And they complained: "we are free." Here they are enslaved, and we thought we were free. We are Americans, we are free. To what extent are we free? You can't pay the rent or buy the food, and we think we are free. I can only be free if I know the art of forgiving sin, and the only one that can forgive sin is God – and God's name is "I AM."

In this world today, in our wonderful land, there are hundred of thousands in prisons physically—but they are Americans. There are hundreds of thousands who are unemployed, who can't pay the rent. Free? They are Americans. I say go and tell every being in the world the story of God – as told us in both the Old and New Testament – and set them free. They can be free if they know who they are. I must tell them the story. There is not one being in jail tonight, if you ask him who he is and how old he is, he will say: "I am John Smith, and I am. . ." and he will tell you his age. But before all these things, he tells you "I am." I have seen this, you see. It frightens people, as you are told in Matthew 9:8: "When the crowds saw it, they were afraid, and they glorified God, who had given such authority to men."

In San Francisco, when I told this story, a lady who sat in my audience had just received notice from the army that her brother had been tried, court marshaled, and sentenced to six months of hard labor. She went home and said: "If this man is telling the truth, I can set him free." She sat in her hotel apartment where she would see if anyone came in. She lost herself in the imaginal state that the bell was ringing and she ran down the stairs, threw the door open, and embraced a brother who was waiting there. She did it for one solid week. The next Sunday morning, before she came to my meeting, it happened. When she came to my meeting, she could not restrain the impulse to rise and she jumped up in the audience of 1,000 and said she must tell the story, and she told it. He was honorably discharged, though he had been court marshaled and sentenced to sixmonths at hard labor.

Everyone can be forgiven. He is not the same being he was - whatever he did to warrant the court martial - why should he pay the last ounce, if she could redeem him by pulling him out of the state that caused him to do whatever he did. If I am pulled out of the state into another state - if I had someone tonight who was the most horrible beast in the world and I am determined to make hima loving, nice person, then he comes into my world and demonstrates his kindness by his act, by everything - he is not the same being he was when I disliked him- the same immortal soul, but he is in a different state. Always I was judging the state, but should I keep him in that state and make him pay a price that belongs only to that state? You see, there is such a thing in this world as God's mercy. No sins can be expiated unless God intervenes and is merciful - for you are God and you can intervene. He gave it to you. Only God can forgive sin, and you can forgive sin: therefore, are you not he? God is merciful. Can't you be merciful and completely transform any being in the world? And oh! What a thrill it is to transform a being and see them different in a little while!

So I ask you to try it, it cannot fail. But believe the statement in the Lord's Prayer: "Forgive us our trespasses." We have actually trespassed. We have heard a rumor and we got off the beam. We see the signs all over the place: "No Trespassing," but we step upon it. Don't. No matter what you hear of anyone, have no ears to hear it unless it is something lovely, for they are only discussing a state, and they are keeping that being in a state. Don't listen. Pull everyone out, but don't forget to pull yourself out. Put yourself into the most glorious state of being successful, being wanted, being happy. You try it. I promise you it will not fail you.

Now let us go in to the silence

Seedtime and Harvest

As you have been told, this morning's subject is Seedtime and Harvest.

Although it bears the same title as my latest book, it is not to be found in that book, for that book is an attempt to interpret some of the more difficult passages of the Bible. I have given you in the nine chapters a mystical view, and also a certain approach how you yourself may approach the interpretation of the Bible, for, as you know, it is not a book of history. And so, when I became aware of deeper meanings in the passages than those normally assigned to them, I began to see them or to apprehend them mystically, and so I have given you a mystical interpretation of many of the darker passages.

For instance, when Solomon made himself a chariot of the wood of Lebanon, he made himself — no one made it for him. That's what you must do — that's what I must do — that's what everyone must do — and in that chapter, I showed you the wood is not wood as you know wood. It means the wood of Lebanon is the incorruptible mind. But you make it for yourself, and we showed you the sides, what they were made of and what the meanings really are.

Then we took that very strange passage, the instruction to the Disciples to take off their shoes or provide no shoes when they travel, and we showed you the word "shoe" is not just the thing I wear on my foot; it is the symbol of the spirit of 'let me do it for you'. For the shoe takes upon itself not only the dirt and the muck that would normally fall upon the wearer's foot, but it protects the wearer from any contact with the outer world, and so anyone who offers to do for us what we should do, and could do far better ourselves, is offering himself as our shoe, and if I would awaken spiritually I must do it for myself.

I must take my own mind and control it — take my wonderful imagination and actually control it and set it to noble purposes and not have some intermediary come between myself and God. For the God of this world is an internal God. He is that inevitable force that expresses in outward facts the latent tendencies of the soul, and so, if I would discover that God I cannot have you do my work for me. I cannot have you eat my spiritual food and expect to grow spiritually. So that is really the attempt of the nine chapters in the book "Seedtime and Harvest."

But this morning's subject — I want to approach it differently. This statement is taken from the Book of Genesis, the 8th chapter of Genesis — it is a promise made to man that "while the earth remaineth, seedtime and harvest, hot and cold, summer and winter, day and night shall not cease." We are told that man was placed in a garden — the garden was completed — every tree was bearing fruit

— everything in the world was finished — and he was placed in the garden to dress it and to keep it. He doesn't plant it, he doesn't do a thing but dress it and keep it. He is not called upon to make trees or to grow new trees — everything is finished!

As we are told in John — "I have sent you to reap that whereon you bestowed no labor"— for Creation is finished. Every conceivable human drama, every little plot, every little plan in the drama of life is already worked out, as mere possibilities while we are not in them, but they are overpoweringly real when we are in them. So man can get in touch with that particular state of his choice, for my imagination can put me in touch inwardly with the state desired so I and in it. If I am in it I will realize it in my world. The states in which we find ourselves are the seed time. The harvest is simply the encountering of events and circumstances of life.

But man's memory is so short he forgets the seedtime, but all ends run true to origins, so if the origin, say is misfortune the end will be misfortune. But when you reap misfortune, you wonder "Why should it happen to me? When have I set a thing like this in motion? Haven't I given to the poor? Haven't I attended service? Haven't I prayed daily, and why should these things happen?"But you see my God never forgets because He always gives the end in harmony with the origin, and you and I are selectors: we don't make; we are not creators; — creation is finished, the whole vast world of creation, as told us in Ecclesiastes "I am the beginning and the end. There is nothing to come that has not been and is." So look upon creation as finished — and you and I are only selectors of that which is. By selectors I mean that you and I have the privilege (we may not exercise it) but it is our privilege to select that aspect of reality to which we will respond, and in responding to it, we bring it into existence for ourselves. Not knowing that we are so privileged, we simply go through the world reflecting the circumstances of life, not realizing we have the power to create or to out-picture the circumstance of life.

So now let us now analyze what I personally mean by seedtime. If everything is finished and completed, then why the promise there shall be seedtime and harvest as long as the earth remains ? Now seedtime, to those who are here this morning, as we should really know, we are not taking it literally, our seedtime is that moment in time when you and I react to anything in this world. It may be to an object, it may be to an individual, it may be to a bit of news that we have overheard, but the moment of reaction, that emotional response, is our attitude. Our attitudes are the seed times of life, and although we may not remember the seedtime or the moment of response, nature never forgets, and when it suddenly appears in our world, that suddenness is only the emergence of a hidden continuity. It was continuous from the moment of reaction until it appeared in the world.

Its appearance in the world is harvest so you and I may harvest anything we desire but we must first have a seedtime. It must be preceded by a moment of response or an attitude. How often you say, "I approached it in the wrong attitude" or "He is in the wrong attitude" or "You must change your attitude if you would get on in this life." I have said it — you have said it — maybe we have said it to each other — but we know the importance of right attitude. We know this much: that I can change my attitude if circumstances change — that's automatic. We know that if something happens suddenly in my world of which up to that moment I was not aware, I, becoming aware of a change of circumstance would automatically produce in myself a change of attitude. We all do that, morning, noon and night, but that's not important, that is a reflect of life. Ninety-nine percent of the world reflect life.

Now, can I consciously, can I voluntarily, can I deliberately produce in myself a change of attitude, one of my own discretion, one that I myself single out, and not one that is determined by or in any way is dependent on a stimulus of a change in the object itself. Must you change before I will change my attitude towards you? We know that if you do change I will change my attitude towards you, but must I go through life simply reflecting these changes in the objects, and can I not deliberately determine the change prior to the change in the object?

For if I can, I am moving towards complete control of my fate and becoming the master of my fate if I can assume an active, positive attitude and not depend upon changes in the object for changes in myself. If I can do it, I really am, if not a complete master, I am becoming more in control of the circumstances of life, but ninety-nine percent of the world waits for things to happen on the outside and then they reflect; that's no accomplishment at all. If we would awaken and become real selectors of the beauty of this garden that God gave us so that we can single out that particular aspect to which we will respond, then we will do it by deliberately changing our attitude towards life itself.

There is a little fable given us to show us how it is done. If you will study the fable carefully, you will see the importance of imagination. The fable is the fable of the fox and the grapes. You all know it. When he failed to obtain the grapes then he persuaded himself that the grapes were sour, and by imagining the grapes to be sour he evoked in himself a change of attitude. He no longer felt about the grapes as he formerly felt. Now that's a little fable on a negative tone or a tragic tone. You and I take the same story but now we put it on a positive tone. We contemplate our ambitious dream, our noble concept of life. It may seem we haven't the talents to realize it – instead of saying what the fox did, that the thing is beyond us and therefore it is sour anyway, we can take the same technique and wonder what it would be like had we realized it. What would the feeling be like were we – (and we name it) – if I can contemplate what the feeling would be like were I the man that I want to be, were you the person that you want to be, and rejoice in that state as though it were true, I am producing in myself that emotional response necessary for seedtime.

I may not see an immediate harvest, maybe the thing that I am now giving expression to in the form of seedtime is an oak, it is not a little mushroom that would grow overnight. Maybe my dream would take a little longer interval of time between the actual planting and the reaping, but if I know that all these things are consistent, – "See yonder fields! The sesamum was sesamum, the corn was corn. The Silence and the Darkness knew! So is a man's fate born" – so, if that moment of response is the actual planting of the seed, and if it was corn, it must be corn when it appears in harvest time, then I can select the nature of the things I want to encounter in my world. I can take not just Neville as a man, I can take the request first ofmy circle, my intimate circle, as a family man – my wife's desires for her child, for her husband, for herself – the child's desire for itself – and move beyond my little circle as a family man into the circle of friendships, move beyond that into my acquaintances, move beyond that into total strangers, impersonal states, but if I know the law holds good, no matter when I operate it, if I do it unconsciously or consciously, you get results regardless, and the results are in harmony with the planting, with the actual seedtime.

Now what is now our seedtime today. There are maybe two thousand odd here, we have two thousand odd different requests, multiplied by a large number because we have requests for others but you can take, today, as you sit here and you can actually contemplate what it would be like – suppose it were true. Suppose I could turn now to a friend and rejoice with him because of his good fortune and actually carry on a mental conversation with him from the premise that he or she has already realized the dream. Now as I do it in my imagination I am setting up within myself a certain changed attitude in regard to that individual. I am producing within myself a certain positive, deliberate, emotional response, and that very moment that I do it, is seedtime. I will encounter that individual tomorrow or next week or next month and he will bear witness of that thing I plant now.

He may be totally unaware that I planted it in this garden. I am not seeking his praise, I am not seeking credit – I am seeking results. If I see the man become the embodiment of the success I know that he desires and I desire for him, that's praise enough, that's payment enough. What more payment would anyone desire other than the results, for everything is a gift. Why should I be given more! My Father gave me the garden — the whole thing is in complete and full bloom and gave me choice — the greatest gift of all, complete freedom of choice of the nature of the fruit I will reap in my world; but I cannot just barge into the garden and start picking fruit — there must be a seedtime, but I must always bear in mind I will reap that whereon I bestowed no labor. I don't labor to make it so, I simply plant it, for in that moment of response is contained all the plans, all the energy necessary to unfold that plan into a perfect wonderful objective fact which I will then harvest by becoming aware of it as an external reality, but I don't labor to make it so; I simply must know it is so.

So that is our privilege, that is our choice. If you believe it, aren't you amazed at the kind of things that you planted, at the kind of seedtime that in our ignorance, in our sleep, we allowed to actually scatter in our world? You see some will say, "But why does God allow it?" You cannot conceive of an infinite God that is not infinite in every respect. If I was incapable, actually incapable of assuming, say, an unlovely state, I could not be my Father's son because my Father is infinite, and if He were actually incapable of assuming any state then He would not be God. Everything is within me — but everything. You cannot conceive of something that I don't contain — the most horrible thing in the world were it not so I could not be infinite, and, therefore, not the son of my infinite Father. So God is infinite and gave us everything, but He gave us freedom of choice that we may become selective, discriminative and bring out everything that is beautiful out of that garden. If I took the piano, the eighty-eight notes of the piano, if I could extract from that piano keyboard every discord, I would not have a piano keyboard. If I could strike a discord and because it frightens me or it disturbs me, the thing grates upon my nerves; if I could now extract the notes that produce the discord and then keep on extracting the notes that produce the discord, I would remove the eighty-eight notes — there would be no notes left on which I could play tomorrow's harmony. But let me leave the notes and learn the art of playing the piano so I can fromthe same eighty-eight notes bring out all the harmonies of the world.

The same thing is true of man. Instead of looking at someone and accepting as final the evidence of the senses; there is someone who brought out into his own world, say disease: he is trying to analyze it from the outside — when did I contract the bug, when did I come in close contact with someone who had the bug and they are taking me into the laboratory with my blood and try to find it there. You will never find it there, in spite of all the wisdom of man. You will find it only in the consciousness of the individual, who, at a moment now long forgotten, planted the thing he is now harvesting — and you are not going to find it in any external analysis at all because things seen were never made of things that do appear. You are warned time and time again in all the books of the Bible, but especially in that 11th chapter of the Book of Hebrews, that "things seen were not made of things that do appear" but no man believes it.

He insists on finding it in things seen, so he extracts my blood, he extracts a little piece of my skin, and he starts to make an analysis of that, and he will tell me yes, he has found it. It's in my blood. I am not denying he has found it in my blood, but why is it in my blood ? It is in my blood or in my body, or in my world because at some point in time, I, exercising the right as a free child of God, singled out some unlovely state relative to another. It need not be to myself; it could be to another, wherein I rejoiced in the hurt of another; where my emotional response to the news I heard was "good" so, I set it in motion, but when it happened in my world, I did not think it was so good but it was my harvest — and all these things are the harvest of things you and I have planted; for all things run true to form. Don't be surprised at the suddenness in our world — someone is ill — it is only sudden because we have forgotten, and man's memory is very, very short.

You know that lovely little poem of George Meredith: Forgetful is green earth; The Gods alone Remember everlastingly; they strike Remorselessly, and ever like for like. By their, great memories The Gods are known.

If man could only remember these moments of seedtime, he would never be surprised when the harvest appears in his world. But because he has no memory as to that moment in time when he dropped that seed, which is simply his emotional response to something he contemplated, something he overheard, something he observed, at that moment the thing was done; he didn't have to labor to bring it to harvest — he simply encountered it as something already full grown, so he reaps now that on which he bestowed no labor, outside of choice. He selected it by his attitude, by his reaction.

Now, am I responsible for others in my world? I certainly am! When I take my little mind, my little imagination and think because it's mine — my Father gave it to me, that I can simply misuse it, it isn't going to hurt another. I tell you you do have to use more control for the simple reason I am rooted in you and you are rooted in everyone and all of us are rooted in God. There is no separate individual detached being in my Father's Kingdom. We are one. I am completely responsible for the use or misuse of my imagination.

Do you recall seeing on TV, a dramatized version of the sinking of the Titanic? Do you recall it? Have you read the book. "A Night to Remember"? Well the book itself is by Walter Lord: but 14 years before the actual harvest or that frightful event of the sinking of the Titanic a man in England wrote a book. He conceived this fabulous Atlantic liner and there he built her just like the Titanic, (only the Titanic was not built for 14 years) but he, in his imagination, conceived the liner of 800-ft. She was triple screw, she carried 3000 passengers, she carried few lifeboats because she was unsinkable; she could make 24 knots; and then one night he filled her to the brim with rich and complacent people, and on a cold winter night he sunk her on an iceberg in the Atlantic. 14 years later the White Star Line builds a ship. She is 800 ft., she is a triple screw, she can make 24 knots, she can carry 3000 passengers, she has not enough lifeboats for passengers but she, too, is labeled unsinkable. She is filled to capacity with the rich, if not complacent, but the rich, because her passenger list was worth in that day, when the dollar was one hundred cents, two hundred and fifty million dollars was the worth of the passenger list. Today it would be a billion dollars. All the wealth of Europe and the wealth of this country was sailing on that maiden voyage out of Southampton. Five nights at sea in this wonderful glorious ship and she went down on a cold April night on an iceberg.

Now that man wrote a book either to get something off his chest because he disliked the rich and the complacent, or he thought it might sell or he thought this is the means of bringing him a dollar as a writer. But, whatever was the motive behind his book which, by the way, he called "Futility" to show the utter futility of accumulated wealth, but the identical ship was built 14 years later and carried the same kind of a passenger list and went down in the same manner as the fictional ship. Is there any fiction? There is no fiction! Tomorrow's world is today's fiction. Today's world was yesteryear's fiction — the dreams of men of yesteryear. Wouldn't it be wonderful if I could talk with someone across space and just use a wire? And I couldn't see that one: it would be a mile away beyond the range of my voice — then maybe five miles and maybe a thousand miles — fantastic dreams — then they came true. When they came true, suppose I could do it without the means of a wire. And it came true; suppose now I could do it not just in an audio sense but in a video sense. Suppose I could be seen? And that came true, but when they were conceived, they were all fictional, all unreal.

There is nothing unreal, because God is infinite, and God has finished creation. You cannot conceive of something that your Father has not only done and conceived of it, it is worked out in detail, in all its ramifications. You and I are only becoming aware of increasing portions of that which already is. We are not making a thing — we are discovering God's wonderful world. But now in this church — at least here it should be done, for this is a church of the mind: this is Science ofMind, where there is a science to planting and you do it in a certain scientific manner. You just don't walk the street and reflect; read the papers and reflect — you go out a more positive person than people who gather in similar areas, for the simple reason they go just to hear a service and to be told how bad the world is.

You're not coming here to be told how bad the world is, for if you believe it is bad, there is something you must do about it because you have planted the world. You have your seedtime. So here people gather to be told how to operate this wonderful gift that the Father gave them. There is this wonderful mind and imagination. So you are told to go out and be choosey in your selection; single out that aspect of reality to which you want to respond, success, health, dignity, nobility, something wonderful that you contribute to the good of the world. As you walk by you are contributing to society, you contribute to the community in which you live, not necessarily by giving dollars but you contribute by your wonderful seedtime. If, in your community, you see the need of maybe a church, you see the need of some wonderful school, you don't wait until people get together, you actually, in your mind's eye, contemplate the joy that is yours because of the wonderful school here for the children, a wonderful church here to lift man spiritually, and you wonder what it would be like were it true; — you feel the thrill of witnessing it within. That is seedtime. Then in a way that you do not know and you need not labor to produce, you will encounter that school and that church and these lovely things in your community.

So you plant the seed and let others, who think that they are bringing it into being, let them think so. You go about this world planting the good — that is why you are here. We are gathered here on Sunday mornings to discover more and more about this wonderful gift that God gave us, that we may single out all the lovely things in the world and bring them to birth in our world;

This morning you take not only yourself — start with self — then turn to a friend in your mind's eye, and congratulate him on his good fortune — congratulate him on his expansion in his world, and actually feel the thrill of such contact — at that moment of response that was a changed attitude in regard to that friend— at that moment you planted. Now, in a way you do not know and you need not know, that seed is going to go through its normal natural hidden passage and appear as a reality in your world. Then you will know the power latent within you and you will stop reflecting life and you become one what I call a true creator in the sense that—I mean creator — that you are creating by selecting wise, wise, lovely things in this world and giving them expression in this world of ours.

So that's what I mean by seedtime and harvest; the importance of the right attitude: and you can do it, you need not wait for circumstances to change, you need not wait for the stimulus of a change in the object to produce in yourself the change of attitude. In your office, does the boss act in a rude way towards you? Well then what would it be like if he now saw in me the lady, the helpful person that I really am, or want to be. Suppose he saw in me someone he could praise for my work and raise me in the salary world, give me an increase in salary because of my added effort; suppose he could see that in me, well, contemplate the boss seeing that in you as though he saw it and rewarded you with an increase.

That moment is the moment of planting. It may not come tonight, it may not even come this week in the paycheck, but it will come. You simply keep on planting the lovely things; but if every day when you leave the office you say, "What a skinflint," and you go home and you discuss him with your mother or your husband or someone else, and they sympathize because they really believe you, for they are playing the same reflective, negative approach to life; but if as you ride home or walk home, you walk in the attitude that he had done it — he had increased your income, he had praised your work, and day after day, in spite of other things to the contrary, you persist in it, do you know he will do it? You will produce in him the change of heart because you first produced it in yourself, and he will see in you qualities that he cannot now see, and then your whole vast world begins to blossom— you do it in every sense of the word. You know someone who is lonely — one who really should be happily married in this world. What would it be like if you were told, not by the individual necessarily, but by a third party of the good news concerning John, concerning Mary or someone else. Someone desirous of a lovely home and a gracious home. What would it be like ? Don't be envious. Try to rejoice. Feel the joy that is theirs, and that moment is seedtime for them. They will harvest it — and that is our opportunity to go through the world planting and planting wisely.

Unfortunately, too many of us in church movements — I don't think you will find it in this church — but too many of us in church movements have a very serious attitude towards life. And, of course, the basic attitude is the attitude towards life, not necessarily the individual attitude towards an object or towards an individual, but the attitude itself that the individual adopts through life, towards life, and they have a very serious one. Well, Orage very wisely and very humorously said the serious attitude is this, — they really believe that God has an enormous struggle against helpless odds, and he said that produces in the individual the emotion of "helping poor Father." They go to help poor Father who has created the world and gave it to his children.

Now he brought up another interesting point of the scientific attitude towards life. Having discovered the little molecule or the little atom and the wonderful construction, that is, theoretically — having discovered this wonderful orderly construction of the bricks that make up the world, their attitude is one of orderly insignificance because they believe the world is gradually burning itself out, so no matter how orderly it is, if they really believe the sun will eventually go out and the earth will consume all its resources, what other attitude could they adopt than all dressed up with nowhere to go, because if eventually it is all going to be in nothing anyway, no matter how orderly it is today, it could only be orderly insignificance, but I tell you, as one who has seen beyond the veil, there is no such thing as coming to an end. Life is forever and forever and forever — and forever you are moving up this everlasting pilgrimage revealing the infinite glories of your Father.

So go out wisely today — go out determined to become more selective, more discreet in your choice of ideas you will entertain and single out the idea that would bless an individual and produce in yourself the emotional response that you have witnessed that state in his world, and know at that moment of response, you planted for that individual, and he is rooted in you, there is no such thing as he will not be found in your world for he is rooted in you. Everyone is rooted in you — therefore you will not lose them. It is planted relative to that being and that being is going to harvest it, and you will know the harvest when it appears in his world. You simply plant and let the harvest take care of itself.

Now my time is up.

www.ingramcontent.com/pod-product-compliance
Lightning Source LLC
Chambersburg PA
CBHW021118020426
42331CB00004B/543